AF170731

Petra Schlötzer

Thoughts...

Bibliografische Information der Deutschen Nationalbibliothek:

Die Deutsche Nationalbibliothek verzeichnet diese Publikation in der
Deutschen Nationalbibliographie;

Detaillierte bibliographische Daten sind im Internet unter
http://dnb.d-nb.de abrufbar

© 2013 Petra Schlötzer

Herstellung und Verlag:

BoD - Books on Demand, Norderstedt

ISBN 9-783732-256525

Winter feelings

Last days were very cold at night.
The sun now shines – but shiver
most of the people, when outside they are.
Most have to. See – the river
is almost frozen on its surface.
Looks like in a winter dream.
The coldness has its special grace.
And I feel happy. Cause it seems
as now the winter will come back,
with all its heavy might.
But as I feel – it isn´t so.
Cause spring time is in sight.

Might be that at this very moment
no one else can see that thing.
But in my heart it´s what I feel.
And I look forward – look for spring.
It is already brighter each day –
days are getting longer.
So – don´t be scared – the cold will leave
and everyone feels stronger.

The birds are coming back to stay
and soon we will see green
appearing here from day to day.
And I know this will mean
that everything in life gets warmer,
easier to be done.
No – it´s no need to feel like summer.
Spring time comes. I smell the sun.

Flowers will grow, and bees awake
and everything is rising.
At the moment – it sounds like fake.
But I know – there comes spring.
I also know we need the cold,
the snow and everything
what we have now. So we can see
how wonderful is spring.

It´s getting warmer, brighter, easier,
everything seems nice.
So not just outside – even in us –
let us break the ice.
Let us get warmer, open minded,
more from day to day.
And learn to love all what we have –
in March, April and May.

But not just then of course. No – always –
through whole the year we could
learn being open and rely on mankind –
Yes – I would.

Busy bees

I´m sitting on the Danube river,
watching busy bees at work.
It´s spring, the sun is shining bright.
From far I hear bells of a church.
The bees are busy near my head
in an elder willow tree.
And I just sit here, listening, watching,
thinking how my life will be.

I love the sound of busy bees.
It´s bit like meditative sound.
It´s steady, special, not aggressive,
always there, but never loud.
The bees are busy – on and on –
and I love to watch their action.
Many different girls at work,
no gossip talk. Just satisfaction.

Yes – for sure I cannot really
hear what they are talking there.
But I can feel it – I can listen –
It´s a quiet atmosphere.
Every bee is doing here just
what they know what is their best.
They´re busy, and they seem to love it,
steady forward – not much rest.

So what I learn from watching them
and what I try to talk about,
is – do what you love to do – and steady –
that´s important. And without
watching others – what they´re doing,
or what you think they talk about.
That´s not your business. You are you –
you´re perfect and there is no doubt.

Sometimes I still forget about this, sadly,
and I need a short reminder.
But deep inside I always felt it –
I am perfect – I get kinder,
softer with myself these days.
And I try to stop the pain
that I needed all my life to learn it seems –
now no more pain.

I try to find my way of life now
bit the way I see around me.
Try to live what I can best
and be a kind of busy bee.

What is it that I am meant to be?

This question once more now appears
deep inside my head.
What is it – here and now on earth?
What may be my guiding thread?
What leads me all my life
and what will lead me further?
No one can answer this – it´s me,
my light inside that needs to answer.

What is it that I am meant to be?
It is not "rich" or "well esteemed".
It´s something else – it´s more than that.
Few people know it – how it seemed.
I feel that I am meant to be
a special and a lucky wife.
To feel this needed real long time.
My life felt like a one-way-drive.

But to be honest – yes that´s it.
It´s showing only one direction.
No matter how it feels sometimes.
It´s the one way – it is my lection.
My life is flowing every time –
and I am deep inside that flow.
But some days I can´t feel this way.
I struggle, fight. I can´t let go.

These are the days when I am afraid.
It needs a lot of will and power
to go on, head high, feels not safe.
It´s scary, hard. I lose my power.

But when I am able to relax
once more no matter how it seems
to be from outside, in my mind,
I can relax again. Then gleams
the sparkling light of love and trust
again there in my eyes.
Then I am calm again and ready
for the next step. No disguise.

What is it that I am meant to be?
I did not answer yet the question.
I am exactly that – each day –
I am meant to learn a lot. No question.
But deep inside I really know
what is it that I am meant to be.
It´s happiness, it´s joy and love,
it´s peace of mind – that great big ME.

I am meant to realize right now
that there´s no reason to feel fear.
I am meant to give up doubt and anger,
to feel safe and loved – it´s clear.

It is the biggest lesson now
for me not to be scared for longer.
But to feel trust, rely on me –
my soul, the spirit – I am stronger
and I am loved so much forever.
There´s no one, who is chasing me.
The only one who needs to feels this –
this is me – that great big ME.

I am a soul – a shining light –
that made decisions long before
´bout what will happen in this life.
What will I learn – what is the score.

And now I am really deep inside
in that lifelong learning game.
I made the rules – I make my way –
So no one out there is to blame.
It´s me – my way – my learning school.
It´s me, my curiosity.
It´s me, who choose the way to learn –
the hard way – long way. It´s just me.

So now I know this – and I also
need to feel it in my heart.
I need to let go fears and doubts –
to go on playing – out of heart.
I need to trust my life, my way,
and my higher self.
And then I will be able to
enjoy the flow– relax myself.

Nothing happens there around
that I did not plan for growing.
As I feel it now and know it –
all my life was part of showing
that I am powerful and brave,
that I am brilliant beyond measure.
A lot of people out there saw it –
now I also found this treasure.

Now I start to realize that nothing
real will break me.
Everything is just one step
closer to what´s meant to be.

Inner child

Today I feel something inside
wants to be seen so much.
What is it that screams deep inside
and wants to get in touch?

Yes, I still know which voice it is,
and how it will be called.
My inner child, the one I´ve lost –
that´s how it seemed. But that´s not true.

I asked myself what´s going on.
What is it that I feel.
Why I´m so scared, why I´m alone,
no one would hold me. Is it real?

So I asked more and tried to see
what feelings are inside.
Inside my heart, inside my brain.
Why had that child to hide?

What I have found? So many wishes,
needs that never were fulfilled.
Security and being held.
Just being held, without a word.

I found that little girl inside,
I used to be – much years ago.
That girl was scared, and tried to scream,
but no words came out – no, no, no…

I tried to tell my mum
what´s going on so deep inside.
I tried to tell her with my look,
my big wet eyes – I almost cried.
But she felt nothing – couldn´t see
– and so I started… start to hide.

The child inside me seemed to vanish,
never could be lucky then.
It just got quieter, day by day.
It disappeared – was no more seen.

The only thing – this child had learned –
was never to rely on
someone else. Cause this won´t work.
Trust no more – never – you´re alone.

But now – about thirty years are gone –
I learned so much about my life.
And what I´ve learned is I´m the one –
the most important in my life.

I also learned that everything around me
seems to be a mirror.
For me and what I want to learn,
sometimes are bad things in my mirror.

But everything belongs to me
and shows me what I need.
And each day more – I learn to see –
and try to find what I might need.

And so today I found my child,
the inner one – who was alone.
The one that vanished – no one saw it.
But right now – it´s here again.

I found it, talked to and could hold
and cuddle this young girl.
And she could trust – and just let go
her fears, the anger, everything.

I promised this young girl that now
I´m ever there for her.
She never will now stay alone.
There is no need for any fear!

Innocence

There is so much violence
around us in the world.
Anger, fear, so much emotions –
everybody has it heard.
So, what is it that I think of?
What I really want?
I want to help the innocent –
here – and there – beyond.

There is so much innocence
in every children eyes.
They are the ones who trust and love.
They need not to disguise.
The only thing they´re asking for
is someone to rely on.
Someone who holds them when they cry,
who loves them – on and on.

But in the world around us now
it´s "normal" not to see them.
A child? Who cares? There are so many.
One more or less? No theme.
That isn´t my opinion.
And never will it be.
´cause each one has a right to live.
And to be loved – not only me!

I am convinced that every child
who´s born here on the earth
has its own mission. Try´s to learn
exact the right – and is it worth.
Each one is worth to breathe, to eat,
to sing, to joke, to dance.
And most don´t ask for any more.
So please – give them a chance.

A chance to live, and to be held,
and not to suffer without need.
A chance to learn that this big earth
has everything that we all need.
If everybody tries to find
what really is important –
there would be peace inside of us,
and freedom real could start.

If everybody looks inside
and listens what he´s really wanting –
most have to stop what they do now –
and realize that they are hunting
for something they will never find
in money, house or cars.
No – everyone needs love and freedom,
peace inside his heart.

Most have forgotten this for long time.
And so they try to "be someone".
But when they fall, get ill and die –
they feel what they have done.
They feel that they have missed their lives,
those wonderful emotions –
Of being loved, feel free and try
to live their special notion.

So I will do this – live my life –
and also I will learn
to help the innocent to fly –
to live – feel free – their hearts to burn.
Because the children are the ones,
they´re able to set free
the spark which´s deep inside of us –
in you – in everyone – in me.

I found my spark – I am on fire –
I love with all my might.
So I will make the best of it –
the innocence – the biggest light.

Letting go

Right now I´m on a turning point.
A point of no return.
I have to go – and step by step
I will find what I have to learn.
I´m feeling weak, I´m feeling small,
the little girl again.
I am afraid – but have to go –
to see what wants be seen.

I feel like swimming in a river –
without a chance to stop again.
No – no way out now – never more –
I have to swim – no need to mourn.
I´ve learned the last years many times
my lesson it is named "let go".
Let go all fears, let go all dreams,
all thinking – everything "let go".

Let go your needs, let go your friends,
your family, your stuff.
The only thing you should hold on
is you – your soul – your endless love.
You have to feel what you might need,
to trust right on your heart.
You are a soul that makes experience
as a human. Yes, it´s hard.

Living as a human being
is not easy just because
when we´re born we need to forget
almost everything that "was".
We forgot about our soul,
about the shining light of love.
So we have to make our journey –
here and now – and search for love.

But if we search for everything
around us – and material –
we´ll never find what´s going on.
Cause that is not the real
thing that we are looking for.
We´re searching for our home,
the place where we are coming from –
the shining light of soul.

The place where nothing else exists –
but love and shining light.
The place where everyone again
is free – and safe – all day and night.
So I know about these things –
I know that I´m a soul –
which makes experiences with a body.
No – not easy. Sometimes I feel
like a punching ball.

I also know I need to make
step by step on this long way.
I can´t see now where is this place –
I have to go on – it´s my way.
Every time when I am thinking,
so it´s finished – now it´s done –
I know who I am – what I need –
there´s something saying "no – go on!"

I have to move again inside –
to go on at my journey.
And every time there´s something found
inside me which I throw away.
Another dream, another wish,
another fear or an emotion
of which I never thought for long time.
Now it´s here to feel again.
To take a look at it and feel
what does it really mean to me.
And then – the last step – let it go
again – so I can real be free.

Be free and open for the things
that will come on my way.
The bigger picture of my life –
can´t see all pieces if I stay
on the place where I am now –
no I know I have to move.
And I will – let go and walk –
to find what´s there for me – I´ll move…

Who am I?

These days again are quite interesting –
and I have time to think
once more ´bout me, my life, my way
and ´bout my deepest feeling.
Where will I go, what will I do,
what more I have to learn?
And I am calm and listen inside –
know no need now to concern.

My life seems to be crazy sometimes.
Friends they look at me and say
"How can you smile and keep so calm.
I can´t do it in that way"
Why I am calm and don´t look sad –
because I´ve learned a lot.
And every day I learn some more –
so many life-lessons I´ve got.

My lesson now – the last few days –
it is the most important.
I "knew" it for the last few years –
but never I could "feel" it.
The lesson means to trust in life,
to trust my deepest feelings.
Right now I can trust, feel secure,
and want to hold on to this feeling.

I know my life is perfect –
every day I get the things
which I do need, I have to learn,
everything I need for healing.
Sometimes of course it don´t seem so.
It seems that life is hurting me.
Yes - if it hurts, it is a sign –
there is something I have to see.

It´s easier often not to try
to have a look what´s hurting me.
But if you hide and run away –
then life shows harder – till you see.
What life want show me is to see
again that I´m a perfect soul.
I´m living as a human now,
to feel emotions – hot and cold.
The most of us they have forgotten
who we really are –
´cause everyone is light and soul –
a loveable and perfect star.

So I do "know" it now for years –
and I am real convinced of it.
But now I also seem to "feel" it,
have to learn that it´s indeed.
I feel my inner calmness now,
my trust in my own way.
Don´t know where it will lead me –
and also know no one can say.

But what I feel it is I have to
go on my next steps,
which show me which one is the next.
And so my way will get a fact.
I know my way will bring me
to the place I have to be.
The place I´m save, I feel at home –
but where it could be? I can´t see.

I learn to trust my inner wise,
my higher self – how you will call it.
And I am calm and go my way,
bit curious – but not afraid.
I know my love still is an anchor –
which will ever hold me.
I know I´m warm, I know I´m save,
there´s no need to feel fear.

The miracle of life

Life is not easy – sometimes cruel –
but if you see it clear
it all makes sense. No need to mourn,
no need to feel this fear.
My life´s interesting – always changing.
Sometimes I´m in doubt.
Don´t know what I should do right now.
My feelings not allowed.

But what I found each day again –
and I am really thankful –
there´s no mistake in everything
that happens – no, I´m grateful.
I am allowed to see each day
the miracles of life.
To feel that I´m awake and healthy –
have food – can walk – a happy wife.

And that´s the way I want to see it
and also will show others.
We´re rich – no need to mourn about it.
No one here really needs to suffer.
But most can´t see it – never learned
to feel the joy of life.
Never learned to thank for so much
what is "normal" for our life.

Each one has to be like someone
else tells how you have to.
I don´t want this anymore –
so I have to move and to let go.

Let go again some wishes
and some thoughts they´re in my head.
So I will be more open now
and find the steps – my leading thread.

I´m curious about everything,
what will happen next.
I´m also proud ´bout every step –
and feel that all is for my best.
I love my life – and many people
that have come my way.
Most I love me – the girl inside –
she´s with me all time – all my way.

Learning from the river – how to live in flow

I sit there, watching – nothing else –
near the river´s edge.
I do this often – and enjoy
what might happen next.
The water´s flowing. Does not care
of what might come where else.
It´s in the flow – no need to think.
No struggle. Time to rest.

The river – never ends
and no one can say where it started.
It always changes – no time the same –
lives really "open-hearted".
Each situation comes and goes
when it´s the perfect time.
Sometimes in waves – sometimes real slow
and never one straight line.

The water does not fight the whole day
"Is that the right direction?"
"Should I go back to where I came?"
"Knows anyone my mission?"
The water flows – with confidence –
wherever it is guided.
No need to mourn – no need to ask –
be brave and feel delighted.

It also never tries to ask
"Oh – do I like this drop nearby?"
"What might he think – what does he mean?
Shall we both really share the way?"
The water flows – goes on and on –
will never get lost anywhere.
Although sometimes you may not see it –
it´s not vanished – it´s still there.

It flows through high and deeper areas –
up and down all day.
Over the stone – nearby the roots –
whatever happens – it´s ok!
It´s strong – and weak – at the same time.
It´s calm and also noisy.
It comes and goes – just with the flow.
No struggle – passion – and real joy.

I´m also in the flow right now.
Believe in heart and soul.
I don´t forget my brain of course –
but it´s not leader anymore.
I try to live my life from now
a bit the way the river shows.
Be confident and trust yourself.
No need to "do" something – let go.

While being one drop in this flowing
river of this quite big world,
it´s hard to feel alone again.
Why should I? This does not more work.
I´m one – and also part of so much
bigger things around.
Sometimes I can imagine how big –
but there´s no way those things to count.

So try to live the life you´re living
like the waterdrops out there.
They´re happy – curious – childish – strong
and so much more you can read there.
And if you try to force them
to a place they will not go –
don´t wonder if there comes the moment
when united drops will overflow.

The tiger

The last few days have been important.
Once more I must believe
I am sitting in a cage for so long –
like a tiger – cannot leave.
The tiger´s me – that´s how I feel
for so long in my life.
I am strong, I am wild, and I am fenced in.
I dream about my life.

The tiger´s dreaming of a life
in freedom and in peace.
He wants to run, to feel alive
and wants so much release.
It is a curious animal,
it smells the wilderness already.
It teaches others how to get there –
you need to trust – let got – feel ready.

The tiger´s dreaming for so long now
´bout a happy "tigers life",
to run, to play, to hunt, to sleep,
to do whatever is called life.
But now – these days – the tiger feels
that someone wants come near.
Someone who tries to build up trust –
to wash away now any fear.

Someone who tries to come inside
the cage the tiger´s used to.
And so – it feels like harm comes in –
the tiger´s scared. No place to go.
No place inside the cage to escape
this seeming disaster.
What shall the tiger do now?
Oh – where he is the master?

The tiger´s fighting shows his teeth,
he scratches and bites with all its might.
The "enemy" is shocked, stands still.
The tiger seems to win the fight.
But when he realized again
what happened there before
the tiger struggles – am I right?
The enemy said "Here´s the door"?

What if it´s real? What if he wants
only to set me free?
What if there is no harm around?
What if this step might heal me?

The tiger sat down – sad and crying –
starts again to dream
from freedom – peace – and love outside
the cage. There starts to gleam
a spark of trust, and promising
himself to change reactions,
the tiger rests – and tries to wait
for any other action
outside the cage, to show that there
is someone who is able
to open up the door again
to freedom – long and stable.

The tiger knows that he´s the one
to do the step outside…
But still he´s scared a bit of joy
and life and tries to hide.
But there will come the day – where this
scared tiger leaves the cage,
to happiness, to love, to freedom –
feel alive – no thought of age.

Compost – Composed

What is it that I write about today?
Might be interesting.
I´m writing about compost –
´bout harvesting and resting.
Once you started with the process
and you still get deeper,
it´s a special atmosphere.
Not working for a sleeper.

There are a lot of steps to do,
preparing for the end result.
Some of us learned it, others not yet.
Composting inside – as adult.
One might think there´s one recipe
that should work on and on –
but that´s not true – each is unique –
and each must find his own one.

You need to have a look at life,
at all you´re going through,
and realize then – nothing´s waste –
all´s needed – that´s the clue.

You need to lose the fear of darkness,
shadows, anger, shitty stuff.
Cause if you use it the right way, it´s
nurturing – not wasted – and above
you put whatever you can harvest,
greens and grass and shredded wood.
A bit of this, a bit of ashes,
a unique mixture – that is good.

You have to try and make mistakes,
but in the end you find
your unique recipe – that lasts –
and brings the best out – just remind
yourself that all is part of you –
all wants to serve and help you grow.
There is no way for instant growth.
We all start from the ground below.

A tiny little seed is put
into that earth when we were born.
But all our talents, skills and wishes
already exist – but most unknown.
That tiny little seed will try
to find a way into the light,
needs to build roots, to feel the ground,
to find the balance, to feel right.

If I remember now how long
it took me building roots,
to find out that I stand real strong,
sometimes too stiff, the balance lost.

I have been struggling quite long time
to come out of the soil,
but now I am through the darkest part,
start seeing light and feel the flow
of life around me and inside.
It´s such a precious feeling.
I feel alive – go on to grow –
to blossom. That feels very healing.

So just remember how important
it is to use all of your stuff.
Whatever experience you have made,
it´s worth to use it – though it´s rough.

If you have found the mixture of
how to put your things together,
you need some moisture, air and warmth,
not too much pressure – mixed together.
Then´s time to rest and to be patient,
curious about how it works out.
And once the time is over –
you can bring your compost out.

You can start growing flowers,
or everything you want to grow.
You can support some others who might
garden also – help them grow.

Appreciate all that is needed –
all the seeming "wasted" things.
And be surprised how things work out.
Feel the support of angel wings.

So just remind yourself sometimes
that "shit" is very needed.
And to compose the life's compost
you need a lot of shit – indeed.

Contents:

Page	6	Winter feelings
Page	8	Busy bees
Page	10	What is it that I am meant to be
Page	14	Inner Child
Page	18	Innocence
Page	22	Letting go
Page	26	Who am I?
Page	30	The miracle of life
Page	32	Learning from the river – how to live in flow
Page	36	The tiger
Page	40	Compost - Composed

Petra Schlötzer, * 1975

These poems show a part of my life´s journey. The ups and downs, the thoughts, doubts and fears. But the most they show how I love living and learning on my spiritual path.

Nothing happens "by chance" – and everything is part of my growth, my spiritual lessons. I am very grateful to see life from that perspective.

I am very grateful for family and friends who join me on that path – though it´s sometimes a strange path which I take. But – with them around and the knowledge that they still care – it´s much easier to go on.

I am a journey girl – on the spiritual journey of my life.

Regensburg, 2013

Petra Schlötzer

German books published at Literareon, Utz Verlag München.

„Gedanken für Jedermann"

„Sehr persönlich…"

Poems and stories for everyone to think about…

Published at Books on Demand, Norderstedt

"Was quakst Du denn? Die Kröte erzählt…"

„Was Wichtelkinder wissen müssen"

Fairy tales to look at life from a different view.